In recent years it has become more an
part of the history of jazz is to be foun(
recording studio. The discovery and issue of many broadcast
transcriptions and airshots, and other recordings of nightclub and
concert performances, together with published reminiscences,
throws the life of musicians and their orchestras into fresh
perspective. *Pure at Heart*, a monograph by and about Hezekiah
Stuff Smith, a unique, creative instrumentalist at the forefront of
the development and achievements of swing music, and the
separately available *Stuff Smith Discography (Disc & Tape)*, are
contributions to the recovery of that history.

PURE AT HEART

Stuff Smith at Annie's Room, April 1965

STUFF SMITH
PURE AT HEART

EDITED BY
ANTHONY BARNETT
&
EVA LØGAGER

AN INTERVIEW
WITH THE PARTICIPATION OF
TIMME ROSENKRANTZ

THAT'S THE STORY OF LOVE

THE HUMAN SIDE OF JAZZ
AN AUTOBIOGRAPHICAL
FRAGMENT

TIMME ROSENKRANTZ
REFLECTIONS

A·B

Distributed in the UK by
ALLARDYCE, BARNETT, PUBLISHERS
14 Mount Street, Lewes, BN7 1HL

Distributed in the USA by
CADENCE MAGAZINE
Cadence Building, Redwood, NY 13679

Please address enquiries or information, in
particular about unissued recordings, to
Allardyce, Barnett, Publishers

British Library Cataloguing in Publication Data
Smith, Hezekiah Leroy Gordon Stuff *1909-1967*
Pure at Heart
1. Jazz—Biographies
I. Title II. Rosenkrantz, Timme
III. Barnett, Anthony IV. Løgager, Eva
781.65092

ISBN 0 907954 15 4

Set by A B Composer Typesetters, Lewes
Printed by Laceys (Printers) Hove

NOTE

The previously unpublished 'Interview' with Hezekiah Stuff Smith, including the participation of his friend and sometime manager Timme Rosenkrantz, was recorded at the Regent Palace Hotel, 28 April 1965, a week after the commencement of Smith's residency at Annie's Room, the club owned by Annie Ross. My meetings with Smith, including subsequent meetings in Paris and Copenhagen, were the culmination of some ten years in search of and listening to his music since first coming across four sides by the Onyx Club Boys among a pile of records in a cupboard at home. In the light of later knowledge there are occasions in the interview when the opportunity to delve deeper was missed because salient points were not always recognized. Twenty-five years on I have a better idea about which questions I would like to have asked. I have edited the interview as little as possible. Three dots mark the omission of some few words that are not easily audible (Smith was not close enough to the microphone for every word to be caught clearly when he spoke softly) or questions that are too confused or insignificant. Larger gaps of this nature are mostly described within square brackets, as are explanatory editorial intrusions that seemed necessary or useful. Occasionally, a bracketed question mark precedes a name (or the spelling of a name), not clearly audible on the tape, that I have not been able to confirm from other sources.

'That's the Story of Love' is the title Smith probably gave to his sketch about Adam and Eve. The text printed here is transcribed from a tape Smith made on the occasion of Eva Løgager's birthday in 1966; but the date of composition, apparently in the 1930s, is not known. The conjunction of the names Eve and Eva is quite fortuitous; Smith narrated the story, to great amusement, at Annie's Room.

In 1967, at my suggestion, Eva Løgager began recording Smith's autobiography 'The Human Side of Jazz'. Unfortunately, in the event, only one short tape, in three sections, was made before he died. The introductory character of this fragment should be borne in mind. Even so, Smith recounts some hilarious and fascinating anecdotes and makes pithy observations which show another, more serious side.

The late Timme Rosenkrantz's 'Reflections' is a reprint of an article which he wrote for *Downbeat* 3 January 1963. I have made a few editorial instrusions within square brackets.

Although the quality of the original photographs is poor, and does not warrant fine reproduction, they are reproduced here as contemporary documents of interest. Also included is a checklist of selected issued recordings.

I would like to express my grateful thanks to Eva Løgager for her kindness in helping to gather the contents of this little book by and about Hez, as he was known to his friends.

A.B.

Reliable information about Stuff Smith's life and music has not always been easy to find. Apart from brief, often illuminating, references and anecdotes in many journals, album notes, and books by or about jazz musicians, two readily available sources are Arnold Shaw *52nd Street: the Street of Jazz* (Da Capo, New York, 1977) [originally published as *The Street that Never Slept*], and Stanley Dance *The World of Swing* (Da Capo, New York, 1979), though both contain errors (for example, contrary to Shaw, there is no known second Vocalion recording of 'I'se a Muggin'' with drummer Cozy Cole replacing John Washington). Two books which include analyses and transcriptions of recordings in which Smith participates are Gunther Schuller *Early Jazz: Its Roots and Musical Development* (Oxford University Press, New York, 1968) [but Schuller is surely remiss in giving Smith's presence on Swing Street no more than a cursory glance in his subsequent volume *Swing Era: the Development of Jazz 1933-1945* (New York, 1989) and in not discussing Smith's solo masterpieces of the mid-1940s], and Matt Glaser and Stephane Grappelli *Jazz Violin* (Oak Publications, New York, 1981). Two articles, 'Stuff Smith' and 'Violin', also by Glaser, in *The New Grove Dictionary of Jazz* (Macmillan, London, and Grove's Dictionaries of Music, New York, 1988), though not without error and lapse, affectionately and respectfully give Smith his due critical place in jazz history.

A descriptive *Stuff Smith Discography (Disk & Tape)* is separately available from the distributors (Allardyce, Barnett, UK, and Cadence Magazine, USA).

AN INTERVIEW

WITH THE PARTICIPATION OF

TIMME ROSENKRANTZ

FIRST *I'd like to ask why you decided to play the violin when so many other musicians weren't.*

Well, I figured that, that, I, well, I'll tell you, I, to tell you the truth I, really all I wanted to do was to play the 'West End Blues', just like I told you before, and my father wanted me to be a classical violinist because he had sent my sister to Oberlin Conservatory and she was about ready to graduate, and he wanted her and I to tour all around and play the classics, you know. But I had other little feet than that man [laughter], you know, I didn't dig none of that issue and when I heard Louis [Armstrong] play 'West End Blues' I said now here man you know that's the tone I want to hear, the sound, and the feeling, which made me feel good you know. So I practised for a couple of months or so and Dad didn't know anything about it [laughter], this 'West End Blues'.

Did you think of playing any instrument other than the violin?

Yeah, I wanted to play piano really, that's true, and drums, and, you see, I sawed the neck off his banjo and started beating the drums oh [laughter] you know, took the strings off it, and like the door of my room was off, so he said, now you play this violin. So he stuck it under my chin. I think it was a three–quarter size [laughter]. It was too large for me. [There is a photograph in *Downbeat* 21 October 1946 taken in Charlotte, N.C. during the 1890s of C. T. 'Pappy' Smith holding a flute in the company of two fellow barber musicians.]

Did you hear, apart from your father, did you hear any violinists, when you were young, who influenced you in jazz?

Yeah, yeah, I heard Joe Venuti. Joe Venuti and Eddie Lang. I heard Joe Venuti and Eddie Lang. They came through our city, and they played at a saloon. And Dad says come over here, I want you to hear this violinist, you know, and this guitar. So . . . [laughter] they was playing good jazz. I thought, you know, I don't know exactly what they are doing but I felt it, you know, one of those things. I think jazz is due to the feeling. Same as all music is nothing but feeling, it's the heart, the soul, the mind, and that's what, I guess, life is.

When you left the Johnson C. Smith University [where Smith had won a scholarship] you joined a traveling musical troupe. Do you remember it's name?

Yeah. *Aunt Jemima['s] Revue.* That was the name of the show.

And the other musicians with you?

Well, King Swayze, and a saxophone player named [?]Ikelberger [laughter] . . . He played pretty nice sax, you know, alto sax, and we had a trombone player we called [?]Trombonski [?bumpski] . . .

Did you play for dances, for stage presentation?

Just stage.

No dancing?

No, no dancing.

Were there any blues singers with the troupe?

No, [?]Sammy Lewis was a singer. He was kinda, kinda [laughter] well, he was a singer, yeah. [Sammy Lewis

12

recorded with trumpet player Ed King Swayze for Okey and Vocalion in 1926; however, Sammie Lewis recorded for Gennett in 1923. There are piano or sketch recordings, some unissued, under the name *Aunt Jemima's Revue* from periods before and after Smith's membership. Henry T. Sampson *Blacks in Blackface: a Source Book on Early Black Musicial Shows* (The Scarecrow Press, Metuchen, N.J., & London, 1980) lists the principal cast of *Aunt Jemima's Revue* for 1927 (after Smith left) as including Sammie Lewin [*sic*] and Baby Lewis.]

Then you joined Jelly Roll Morton or were there some other troupes before?

No, I joined Trent, Alphonso Trent, after that. Swayze left the show, and he went and joined Trent, and then he, when he got in Trent, Trent was going in to do a hotel and he wanted waltzes, so he figured that he needed a violin.

What year was this?

Oh, I don't know man [laughter] I don't know man . . . it was after the first world war [laughter] yeah . . . it was back there. [It was 1926.] I joined Trent in Lexington, Kentucky. Then we went to Dallas. We played the Adolphus Hotel for about a year and two weeks. We played the big hotel in Santa Cruz and a smaller hotel in Houston. As a matter of fact we covered Texas thoroughly. The band, then we played, we were playing for dances then. So Trent says Stuff, you, you get in front of the band, you know, Trent was the leader, he was the pianist. Well he, he wanted me out front because I, I just couldn't sit down in a chair and play, you know, I had to stand up and play my violin, you know [laughter]. And then I can look at all the chicks too and so that was real great . . .

But you did play with Jelly Roll Morton?

Well after we left, after Swayze and I left Trent. We left Trent in Davenport, Iowa and then we went straight into New York and joined Jelly Roll. Jelly Roll sent for Swayze, and Swayze got me in with Jelly Roll Morton. And we was playing five cents a dance, a club called, the, uh, Arcadia Ballroom, on 125th and 7th Avenue [?Alhambra: see 'Nightclubs and Other Venues' in *The New Grove Dictionary of Jazz* (Macmillan Press, London, & Grove's Dictionaries of Music, New York, 1988)]. So we played, I played with Jelly Roll for two weeks, and the band was too loud and then I didn't like the way he talked to Chick Webb 'cause I thought Chick Webb was a great drummer, yeah, and Chick had a band at the Savoy, so I figured, man I'm going back to Trent where I can be heard. We didn't have no amplifiers then, you know. You understand? And they play a waltz, and these cats would play a waltz and play 6/8 time instead of 3/4, you know, they, kind of jazz it up, and you couldn't hear the violin, so I said, they don't need me, so I cut out and went back to Little Rock and joined Trent. And from there I stayed with Trent for about six more months and went to Buffalo.

You made some records with Trent.

Oh yes, sure. Yeah, we made those in Richmond, Indiana. [see Gunther Schuller *Early Jazz: Its Roots and Musical Development* (Oxford University Press, New York, 1968) for an analysis of these recordings.]

Can we check the personnel? Does this check with what you remember? In 1928 the band's trumpets were Chester Clark, Irving Randolph.

14

Stuff Smith at Annie's Room, afternoon of 21 April 1965

No, in '28. Yeah, but before that. Now in '27, now let me give you the personnel of the band: on trumpets was Chester Clark, King Swayze and, that was the trumpets, and one trombone, Leo [Snub] Mosley [laughter]. Now on saxophones we had James Jeter, Lee Hilliard, and Hayes Pillars, no, Hayes, yeah, Hayes Pillars. Now that was the reed section. Now, and in the rhythm section we had Brent Sparks on tuba, wait a minute, Brent Sparks on tuba and A. G. Godley on drums and, yeah, [Eugene] Crook, on banjo and Alphonso Trent on piano, and I played the violin.

On the first records Robert Eppie Jackson was tuba?

Eppie, Eppie, from Kansas City.

And when did Irving Randolph join the trumpet

section?

Later, 'cause Swayze went with Cab Calloway, yeah.

And then around 1930 Peanuts Holland joined the trumpets? [In fact, he joined a year or two earlier.]

Peanuts Holland. I got Peanuts the job in the band.

George Hudson?

George Hudson followed Peanuts. When we went back to St Louis and played on, no, we didn't, we played a dance in St Louis and we picked up George Hudson. And George, at that time, he didn't have a band.

Eddie Sherman came in on tenor?

That's when I cut out. See, I cut out then. I went back to Buffalo. I remember that 'cause my wife had a baby [laughter], had to go back to care for my son.

Do you remember the musicians in your Buffalo bands?

Yeah. On trombone . . . I had two of them. What do you mean, my eight piece band?

You had Joe Thomas on tenor at one time?

Yeah, well that was a seven piece band. In my seven piece band at [?]Ann Montgomery's Little Harlem. That was in Buffalo. She told me to bring in a band, and I did, you know, I went out and got some musicians. I had on trumpet, first trumpet player I had was Peanuts [laughter], Peanuts Holland, on trumpet. Joe Thomas on tenor, Al Williams, no, Al Williams came in later after Joe went with Jimmie [Lunceford]. Let me see now. On trumpet I had Peanuts Holland, well I remember James Sherman on piano . . .

You made two more records with Trent in 1933. [No! Smith's last records with Trent were made in 1930.]

But I wasn't in Trent then . . .

With Gus Wilson on trombone?

Well Gus Wilson was in my band.

The titles were 'Clementine' and 'I've Found a New Baby'. With the violinist Anderson Lac[?e]y.

Ah, I wasn't with Trent then. No, no. See Gus Wilson, I got Gus Wilson, that's Teddy Wilson's brother . . . Gus Wilson, good arranger, and everywhere he goes he makes an arrangement on 'Clementine'.

So you're not playing on those two records?

No, no.

After you left Trent and before you made 'I'se a Muggin'' in 1936 did you make any other records?

No, no. My first record [after Trent] was in '36. That was for Vocalion. [In conversation some days later Smith recalled his participation in unissued recordings by Zach Whyte's Chocolate Beau Brummels. The discographical details for this 1931 Gennett session are included in Brian Rust *Jazz Records A–Z, 1897-1942* (London, rev. 5, 1983). Smith remembered the participation of Roy Eldridge and Vic Dickenson (Rust does not list Eldridge but does question the presence of trumpet player Walter Savage) and joined the orchestra for this session only.]

Do you recall the period leading up to your Onyx Club engagement?

Yeah. I played at [?]Ann Montgomery's. And then I, I had a seven piece band there, and then I went into the Vendome Hotel, and then I had a twelve piece band. That's where I, that's when I got hold of Gus Wilson on the trombone. Hm, I've forgotten all the guys' names. I had Jonah [Jones], I had Jonah in the band.

In Buffalo?

Yeah, and we, Jimmie Lunceford told us to come into the Lafayette Theatre [in New York in June 1934], and [?]Harold [?]Oxley was supposed to book us, you know, around the world. Now what we call around the world is New York, Philadelphia, Baltimore, and Washington. That's around the world. In the music game [laughter].

I've seen photographs of you and Jonah at the Onyx Club with a caption which says Jonah's 'truckin'' dance should never have gone beyond his version. What was special about the way he used to do it?

Ah, he had flat feet [laughter] . . .

[Small talk about the personnel of the Onyx Club Boys.]

You wrote 'Crescendo in Drums'.

I wrote that for Cozy [Cole] when Cozy went with Cab [Calloway] [laughter], the dirty dog. I'll never forget

that one. That's when we were in the [?]La Salle Hotel.
[Cole recorded the composition with Calloway in 1939.
When Smith recorded the title for Varsity the following
year the drummer was Herbert Cowens.]

You didn't record again until . . .

Until I got the trio.

*. . . you recorded with Red Norvo [in Chicago in
1944].*

Oh well, I played with Red Norvo, yeah yeah . . . then
I made a couple of records with a girl named Mary . . .
played guitar . . . yeah, Mary Osborne . . . I'd sure
like to hear them . . . [This 1944 Chicago session co-
produced by Leonard Feather for a projected *Esquire*
magazine label was issued by Selmer in France.]

*This was when you formed the trio with Jimmy Jones
and John Levy?*

Yeah.

What led you to form a trio without drums?

Well, I don't know. Everybody was using a trio, you
know, and the loot was getting awful low [laughter]
back in those days, you know what I mean, don't you,
and the loot was getting awful low, so I was in Chicago
and my old lady had just divorced me, and I had me a
new queen, I had a queen but, you know, I couldn't
expose her [laughter], you understand . . . people
would be calling me Don Juan, that's why . . . but I, I
thought it would be best that I get a, strings, you
know, piano is a string, and bass is a string. And, we
never even had a rehearsal. John Levy was, who was a

19

special delivery, a letter carrier in Chicago. And Jimmy Jones played ukulele. I didn't even know he played piano, you know. But he played beautiful chords on the ukulele. So I saw John Levy once there. I went to the Union and the President, says, I asked him, I says, I want to join it, and I want to get a trio, now give me some good men, you know. So he says well we got a good bass player here, he hasn't played for quite a while, he plays piano and bass. And then we have a pianist who's just come out of college, his name is Jimmy Jones. And I said well you tell those guys to meet me at Eddie's Three Deuces. Now, I'm not talking about the old Three Deuces that we had in Chicago. This is the Three Deuces on Wabash.

Still Chicago?

Yeah. So they met me there and I told them, I told them, I said meet me there tomorrow night at nine, at quarter to nine, you must have, wear a black, blue or black suit with a red tie and a white apron and black shoes and, you can go on about the rest . . . I looked at them and they looked at me and I said, well, let's play 'Crazy Rhythm', and Jimmy said, what key, I said B flat. I said take four bars and that was it. We seemed to gel right there. [There is an amusing story about Smith's visit to the Union in Bill Crow *Jazz Anecdotes* (Oxford University Press, New York, 1991).]

To return to the Red Norvo date for a moment. You told me [a week before] the bass player was Oscar Pettiford.

That was Oscar Pettiford.

And I've seen Clyde Lombardi and Slam Stewart named; are these wrong?

20

I, think that was, that wasn't Slam, hm.

Could it have been Clyde?

Could have been. [In fact, it was; his name appears on the labels of the two issued Steiner-Davis discs.] I know it wasn't Slam.

You never recorded with Slam?

No, never. And we're good friends, we have the same name, Leroy, his name is Leroy. Slam Stewart.

Were the recordings for Asch the first with the trio?

Yeah. [In fact, a radio transcription session, and the session with Mary Osborne, preceded the Asch session—see below.]

There seems to be an unissued title; can you remember it?

We made . . . one more. I can't think of what it was.

You recorded those in September '44.

Yeah.

When did you record the V-disc 'Stop-Look' and 'Humoresque'?

Hm, that was back in New York.

The Asch titles weren't New York?

Hm? Oh, we made those in Chicago. Yeah. [Smith is mistaken: the Asch session was recorded in New York

Stuff Smith and Doug Dobell at Annie's Room, 21 April 1965

a few days before the V-disc session; but there was an earlier transcription recording in 1943 in Chicago for World Broadcasting. Two titles only were issued on Brunswick in the late 1940s—see below—and the complete session, including incomplete takes, was issued in 1988 on Circle CLP 132.] But the V-disc. I made them when Charlie Barnet was up there [in New York]. We made them there. I was in the army.

That was after the Asch session?

Yeah, sure.

Did you make other recordings for AFRS or for AFN?

Yeah, I think so, but I, I don't remember, but I know I did. Because we were, we were on the, not really the

USO, we were Southern Bonds, you know. We sold lots of bonds in Chicago. War Bonds. I don't remember. [Smith made concert and studio radio recordings, including those for Jubilee and Downbeat, which exist on 16" transcription discs.]

You composed 'Stop-Look' on the way to the studio?

Yeah, walking down the street.

Someone nearly knocked you over?

Yeah.

And later in 1944 you made some records for Savoy which were never issued?

Yeah, with Billy Daniels. [One title, 'Always', was issued]. Then I made one for Musicraft with Sarah Vaughan [Smith's composition 'Time and Again' in 1945.]

Any more at that time with Billy Daniels?

I think we did 'Intermezzo', yeah. [Three titles, without Daniels, of the five or six recorded at this session, one with vocalist Rosalie Young, were issued in 1977 on the anthology Savoy (dbl) SJL 2224 *The Changing Face of Harlem, vol. 2*. There are no details in the Savoy files of a recording of 'Intermezzo', a feature for Smith and Daniels in nightclubs, although the matrix following 'Always' has no title allocated. Two titles without Daniels, including one not issued on LP, were allocated a 78 catalogue number which, although cited in *Grove*, is believed to be unissued.]

[Small talk resulting from confusion about two New

York Concerts, one with Jimmy Jones, one with Billy Taylor, in the mid 1940s. Recordings, some of which were issued, were made at both concerts.]

Can you remember any other records you made during the 1940s?

Well, I can recall recording but, in Chicago, with the trio again, but I don't know what company and I don't know what I played. I remember we had a couple of sessions there, on top of some great big old building out there, I've forgotten. [One is surely the World transcription recording.]

You broadcast regularly during this period?

Oh yeah, every night. We were on the air seven o'clock, seven, coast to coast.

Your own shows and other people's shows?

Yeah, yeah, but mostly our shows. We started, we stayed there a year then, we did pretty fair . . . ['Chicago Band Briefs' in *Downbeat* 1 July 1944 reported 'Late radio listeners are catching the broadcasts over WBBM from 1.30 to 2.00 ayem from the Downbeat Room of the Garrick, with the Red Allen–J. C. Higginbotham band and the Stuff Smith trio doing the sending . . . Walter Fuller . . . shares the airlane with Stuff Smith on Thursday nights . . .']

[Small talk.]

You've expressed great admiration for Duke Ellington and you've often recorded his compositions.

Yes, yes. I, well his compositions there's a lot of,

there's a lot of something that, that will live, probably
for ever, you know like the big composers. I put him
in that class. Jazz speaking, and otherwise, Duke writes
[laughter] practically anything you want to write,
according to how Duke feels, I imagine. We'd never
really sit down and talk but we've been pretty good
friends for years . . . yes, I have played with Duke.
[See 'The Human Side of Jazz'. Two titles from a 1945
jam session with Smith and Ellington (though not his
orchestra), reputedly recorded at the Onyx Club, are
included on Jazz Archives JA 35 *Ben Webster and the
Boys—Ben Webster in Small Group Performances*
issued in 1976.]

*Have you played duets with Ray Nance and the Duke
Ellington Orchestra?*

Yeah, at the, I played, well, I played [laughter] Ray and
I, we always jive around, but we played Monterey
Festival together and we played in New York. [And in
Copenhagen.]

*Timme Rosenkrantz issued a recording with you and
Lucky Thompson and Erroll Garner [and George
Wettling] entitled 'Test Pilots' which he recorded in his
apartment.*

. . . and I made a record with this girl that sings . . .
Annie [Ross] sings just like her, I mean she's got the
same style, this girl, she come out with the Five Spirits
of Rhythm . . . a white girl, she sang beautiful, man,
she swung like mad. She never got the breaks she
should have had, a pretty short girl. [Ella Logan, Annie
Ross's aunt; the session is lost—see below. In 1937
Smith and the Onyx Club Boys travelled to Hollywood
to work on the film musical *52nd Street* in which Logan
shared star billing. Smith's performance was not

included in the released print.]

In the late 1940s Brunswick issued a recording: a version of 'Desert Sands' coupled with 'I Don't Stand a Ghost of a Chance'. But this wasn't recorded as late as then?

No, we recorded it way before that.

With Jimmy Jones. Do you remember which session this was? [It was the World transcription session.]

No. No I don't. How do you get all this information [laughter]?

There are books with some of this information. But much of it is inaccurate.

But that's true.

[Small talk about an erroneous journal reference by Stanley Dance to Smith's presence on recordings from the 1940s by Earl Hines; the violinist was Eddie South.]

In 1951 you recorded with Dizzy Gillespie. [And again in 1957.] What were the circumstances?

Well Dizzy came after me [laughter]. I knew Dizzy, you know. I knew Dizzy in New York.

What was your reaction to the young modern musicians, Dizzy Gillespie, Charlie Parker, during the mid-1940s?

Well, at that time I thought they was very, very foolish. Because they were playing, playing notes that, that didn't fit in the cycle of, of chords [laughter],

Stuff Smith and Anthony Barnett at Annie's Room, 21 April 1965

you know, they was just playing all around the chords, in the chords, out the chords.

But your music, your own music, was revolutionary. You played unusual things.

Yes, but, it was always, I'd fall back in that chord somewhere [laughter], you see, these cats would get out of that chord and stay out there, you know. And they called it bebop [laughter] . . .

And later you came to like it?

No. I never did like it.

[Despite these protestations Smith and Gillespie were close. *Downbeat* 29 July 1946 carries a photograph

27

(Smith is in the forefront) with the caption '52nd St. Stars Give Dizz's Band a Send-off: Informal send-off for Dizzy Gillespie's new big band recently on the stage of the Apollo theater found such notables as violinist Stuff Smith, guitarist Tiny Grimes, clarinetist Buster Bailey, trombonist Trummy Young and bassist Slam Stewart sitting in on a jam session that had the Harlem house, scene of many such bashes, leaping. It was a royal send-off indeed for the Dizz and his new crew of re-bopists.']

But you recorded with Dizzy?

Yeah, but Dizzy didn't play no bop then, not when I recorded with him. 'Cause I made the arrangement on 'Caravan' that he, that I made with him [in 1951], and they played very fine. He had the bass player with the Modern Jazz Quartet . . .

Percy Heath.

Yeah. And then he had this other guy who plays vibraphone . . . yeah, Milt Jackson was playing piano.

And he played organ [and sang] on one track 'Time on My Hands'?

Oh, probably so. I didn't play on that, did I?

Yes.

Yeah? Maybe I did. See, there you go, you see.

[Small talk.]

There are very few recordings by you during the early 1950s. There's the New York Phythian Temple concert in 1953. Nothing else until you recorded with Ella Fitzgerald in 1956. What were you doing during those years?

Playing around, fishing, having a ball [laughter].

You were on the West Coast by 1956?

Yeah, I got married, that's what messed things up, I, I, wait a minute, Arlene, I didn't mean that baby [laughter]. I mean, oh dear, I got married [laughter]. [Smith's [?]second wife joined him in Europe not long after this interview but they eventually separated with the intention to divorce. Later, Smith met Eva Løgager in Denmark with whom he remained until his death.]

*Did you enjoy recording [*The Duke Ellington Song Book*] with Ella Fitzgerald?*

Oh, very much, very much. She's as sweet as she can be. And Ben [Webster], and Ben played something fine, and Paul Smith and, who was the drummer?

Alvin Stoller.

Yeah, right, he plays real great, man, he's got a beautiful beat. He don't lose no tempo, hm. And the bass player was great. I've forgotten the bass player's name but he's a good man.

Joe Mondragon.

Yeah, that's him, an Italian fellow . . .

About a week later you recorded with Nat Cole.

Ah, there was a session! There's a boy, man. He can

29

play all the piano you want to hear . . .

And Lester's brother Lee Young was on drums.

Yeah, he played beautiful. I mean to me, you know. Some guys just kind of fit you, you know, and other guys just don't fit you. But he fitted me, and I, what the hell, they don't have to fit me, let me fit them, man! The way they was playing, you know, go, man, shoot. Nat King Cole was one of the finest piano players in the country. I mean, for swinging, man. And, you know, he had so much in his heart, man. Nat really didn't want to sing [laughter] he wanted to have a group. Nat wanted to play piano, I think! I might be wrong. Commercially speaking, it was a good thing he sang, you know, to make some loot. Well, loot's great. All I want is enough loot to just be comfortable, you know, get what I want, you know, I don't want too much, you know, I just want to get me, what I want, you know, maybe a couple of suits or something, to look decent when I walk out, and if I want to buy my friends a little, a dinner, or something like that, I ain't going to say no . . . which would spoil my appetite. But that's all, that's the way King Cole was, you know. I think he was that way. And, by the way, John Levy used to handle King Cole before he even got out of high school [laughter]. So John Levy was a hell of a manager, and he still is. If I could think of this girl who sings in America now that's real tops, she's the top singer now, John Levy's got her, what's her name?

Nancy Wilson?

Nancy Wilson, that's who I'm talking about. That's the top singer in America.

[Timme Rosenkrantz enters.]

Timme Rosenkrantz takes a bow at Annie's Room, 21 April 1965

When did you first visit New York?

R: 1934.

And when did you first meet Stuff?

R: I guess it must have been . . . 1936. He was at the Onyx at the time.

You spent a lot of time around 52nd Street?

R: Well in those days I spent more time uptown because I was living there. And that's where everything happened. The Onyx was the only place downtown really where they had good music, you know, except for the dixieland bands, you know, which were all right if you like that kind of music, which I did when I could have my beer with it. Dixieland and beer go very well together.

S: But the best joint to go to was after the Onyx closed, was Timme's house . . .

R: You say joint? . . . my apartment . . . My home! Not a joint!

S: All the musicians used to say let's go to Timme's, that's all we had to say, and then about twenty of us would go to Timme's. And we used to drink Pernod and drink, er, other things, and eat and Inez [Cavanaugh, who sang and who was Rosenkrantz's companion] would fix us some fine spaghetti and hamburgers, and Timme would be back there recording. You understand me [laughter]?

R: Yeah . . .

[laughter]

S: What's that girl's name that I made those records with and you lost?

R: Ella Logan.

S: Ah, there! Ella . . .

R: Ella Logan.

S: Yeah, that was a singing little girl . . .

R: . . . she was a real, variety, you know, artist, a real artist, you know . . . entertainer . . . She never did much recording, I don't know why because she was, she was tops . . .

s: That's what I'm trying to tell him now. Ella Logan was something else.

Ella Fitzgerald sang with you at the Onyx?

s: No, I had Billie Holiday [see contemporary issues of *Downbeat* and John Chilton *Billie's Blues: a Survey of Billie Holiday's Career 1933-1959* (Quartet Books, London, 1975) for an account of this brief and unfortunate association. But ten years later, in 1946, they were happy to work alongside one another at New York's Downbeat Club.] . . . Ella used to work for me on that program, you remember Timme . . . they had Edgar Sampson part of Cab's band part of Chick's band and my rhythm section, with Jonah . . . [see 'The Human Side of Jazz'.]

R: Well, I wasn't there at the time I think.

s: . . . [?]Thompson . . . [?]Thompson . . . was the Union big boss.

R: I kept going back to Denmark . . . Then I came back in '39 and stayed all during the war years.

s: We had, we had that whole program for, for about seven weeks, and I had a, I had about a fourteen piece band.

R: One of the best things I ever heard Stuff play was on the Mildred Bailey Show. You know, Stuff was a good friend, of course, of Mildred [he participated in several shows] . . . it's on there, it's on that tape . . . the tape I've just, you've got on your lap. [A magnificent unissued performance of 'Bugle Call Rag', a solo feature for Smith with the Paul Baron Orchestra, broadcast in 1944. A separate performance, believe to

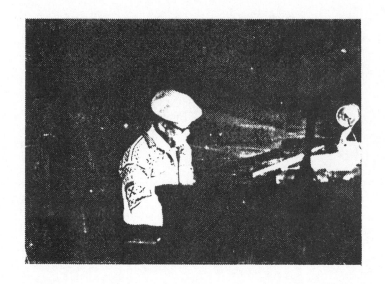

Stuff Smith at the piano at Annie's Room, 21 April 1965

have been recorded at the show's dress rehearsal [but see Timme Rosenkrantz 'Reflections'], or possibly following the show, was broadcast some months later on the Paul Baron Show; it was issued during the 1980s on Swing House SWH 13 *One Deep Breath—Paul Baron and His Studio Orchestra Featuring His Jazz All Stars.* (There is an earlier, inferior issue, without the spoken introduction, on Jazum 3.)]

s: Oh man, you want to hear some violin you must cut this thing off. Now, don't you think that's enough interview?

As you like.

s: All right, now, can I, can I say the ending? May I put the ending on the interview? Tony Barnett, you have really been a very very fine friend of mine in London. Timme and I probably couldn't get along without you, you understand, but I still want to see the Queen's jewels.

I'll take you to see the Queen's jewels.

s: That's good.

R: But, you know, you, you can't take them out with you. You understand that?

s: I didn't, I, I didn't say the *jewels*.

R: Oh.

s: Yeah [laughter].

R: I'll see you later.

Recorded by Anthony Barnett, London, 28 April 1965
Transcribed and edited by Anthony Barnett, September 1990

THAT'S THE STORY OF LOVE

WHEN Adam was in the Goddam' of Edam he was having a ball. He had everything he wanted. He had chickens, gooses, couple of geeses, horses, cows. Till the bull come along. That was competition for the cows. But he had everything he wanted. He even had a little stream that ran through the Goddam' of Edam. And the sun used to shine down on this stream, you know, this little brook, the sun, brook, the brook, the sun, sun, brook, Sunny Brook! Huh. That's a drink they have these days called Sunny Brook. He even had some of that. And every morning he would go down there and get himself a little dipper of Sunny Brook until he drank so much of this Sunny Brook until he got the ulcers. So he decide I better get a new kick. So he looked upon a mountain with his binoculars that he had invented and there he saw Mount Mary's-y'-Mama.

So he ran up to Mount-Mary's-y'-Mama and there was some green grass growing with little brown seeds on it. So he plucked all the seeds off and smashed them all up. Put them in a piece of brown paper he had invented and made him a roach about two yards long. Huh huh. Well, instead of that cat walking over the Goddam' of Edam he started floating over the Goddam' of Edam.

So he floated on back there by the brook and lay down and went to sleep. Finally, he woke up. And there she was. Madam Adam. Miss Eve. She stood over that boy's head and said 'Get up, you square! I'm going to put your boots on and lace them way up to your gills.' Now Adam had never seen nothing like that before. So he jumped up. He said 'Hello babes!' She said 'Now lookey here. You go out to the orchard by that apple tree and when you get there you pluck one of them big apples and bring it back to me.' Adam looked at her straight in the eyes and said 'Ney ney. Forbidden fruit. Forbidden fruit.' Madam Adam said

'Heh heh. Juicy fruit. Juicy fruit.'

So Adam, like a square, went on out there where the apple was parked on this tree. When he got there he saw a great big reptile. A snake. A asp. Well, this ask had his asp wrapped all around this tree. So he looked at him in the eyes. He said 'Adam. Pluck one of these apples. Run up on Mount Mary's-y'-Mama. Get yourself some of that jive. Run back to old Eve and gas that chick.' And that's exactly what he did. Took the apple. Great big red fat juicy apple. Went on up Mount Mary's-y'-Mama. Grab him some of that Mary's-y'-Mama. Ran back to Eva and said 'Pick up, Jack.' She looked at him. Took the apple. Put it in her hand and said 'Adam, are you going to bite this apple this morning?' Adam didn't say a word. She looked at him again and said 'Adam, are you going to bite this apple this morning?' Adam didn't say a word. She said 'Look here, Adam.' She said 'Are you going to stick one tooth in this fine foxy fruit this morning?' Well, did he bite it? Yum yum. Yum yum. Did he bite it? Yum yum. Yum yum. And that's why they leave you, leave you. Leave you with the blues in the night. 'Tain't right. 'Tain't right. 'Tain't right. There you are, Eve!

Written by Stuff Smith, possibly c.*1936*
Recorded by Stuff Smith, for Eva Løgager's birthday, on
or before 15 June 1966
Transcribed by Anthony Barnett, c.*1970*

THE HUMAN SIDE OF JAZZ

JAZZ

AN AUTOBIOGRAPHICAL
FRAGMENT

ALL you fine people. I *hope* that you take time out to read this book that I'm going to try to put down . . .

I love beauty. I don't love sorrow. I love beauty. Beauty. And, when I say beauty, that takes in all the category of music. The sweetness of music. The harshness. The roughness. The anything that you can think of, is right there, in that one word called beauty.

I love beautiful women. Like my wife [Eva], you know. She's beautiful. But she's devilish . . . We're going to show you something that you, I mean we're going to try to show you something in music that probably you didn't know . . .

Number one. I am a violinist. I'm not a fiddle player [laughter]. I'm a violinist. I play violin my way. That's the way I play it. And that's the way I think it should be played. I mean according to my type of music that I play. Now, when I was a young boy my father, who was a musician, my sisters, they were, they were doing pretty good. And I was doing pretty good. So, so, I had my first escapade of hearing some good music, which I love . . .

I love jazz. And they're trying to tear up jazz, trying to make a symphony of jazz. But they can't do it. If you can't pat your foot you ain't got jazz. That's what I'm saying. Now, they've done everything to jazz. They stood still with jazz these days. These boys that are playing. They learn the chorus of a record that some other fella has made and then they come out, and they play that, on their instrument. But don't let them play anything else because they don't *know* nothing else. That's the reason I say good jazz is the jazz that's come from the bottom of the pit. When I say the bottom of the pit that means guys like Joe Venuti. Eddie Lang. Red Allen. Bix Beiderbecke. Coleman Hawkins. Fletcher Henderson. And the old boss, Louis Armstrong. That's good jazz. Frankie Trumbauer. I can name a gang of them. All the boys that play good jazz. And good jazz you cannot beat. If you want to pat your foot. If you don't want to pat your foot go to some symphony [laughter] and listen to Beethoven. He's good too. He *was* good, I mean. But anyway our subject is only jazz. Swing we call it After Benny Goodman. That learned a few licks from our boy in Chicago [? Jimmie Noone] [laughter]. He called it swing. What did I tell you. There's nothing like jazz. It's going to stay here. They're trying to get rid of it. But it's going to stay here. Because it's in your heart. It's in your feet. It's in your blood. And that's the thing that counts. Other things are great. Other things are really great. Like your symphonies give you, give you a menu. I'll say menu. To let you know what's happening. And this and that and the other. But in jazz you just come and sit down and listen. And if it satisfies you, and you pat your feet, that is jazz . . .

Now, you take the case of a young man that I know. A very fine looking little fat trumpet player [laughter]. He's the swingin'est thing on earth. His name is Roy Eldridge. We met years and years ago when I was playing with Alphonso Trent's band. Somewhere in Ohio. He was playing with Speed Webb. And he had *all* of his keys, the top of his keys, taken off. He took them off. And he chopped them down, he chopped down his mouthpiece, to make it real thin, so you get higher notes. And boy, we used to stand back and look at this cat play. Now that boy could play. And now he's turned out to be one of the best in the world. Boy, that's my boy. That's the swingin'est cat in the world. He can swing . . . It don't mean a thing if you ain't got Roy Eldridge [laughter]. That's my boy. That's my buddy.

Now, for instance, you take old [Russell] Procope. Procope who played with John Kirby before. And he played very beautiful. He's a swinging little cat too. All them cats. Cats I'm talking about can swing, man. I ain't bullshitting. I'm talking about the real swing.

Take Jonah Jones. That little old . . . He can swing his ass off [laughter]. He's got a swinging little band. We were together for about seventeen years. From Buffalo. He used to be with Jimmie Lunceford. Then he came over to me, in Buffalo. We had a good little band too. We had us a good little band. You bet your life. Casa Loma boys used to come in and hear it and say, what you doing here in Buffalo? Why don't you go to New York? Why the hell should I go to New York when I live in Buffalo and I'm doing pretty fair? You understand me?

Now, there's another little old boy that can swing his ass off. His name is Peanuts Holland. He's right over here in Europe. He's in Stockholm. Sweden. He played in my band. He could blow like a dog. Yeah, yeah. All of them boys. Vic Dickenson. They all played with me. And I played with them. I mean musically [laughter]. We'll put it that way. I think that's the way to put it. Musically.

Willie Smith. Young man who's just passed away. About a month ago. He was one of my best friends. He was supposed to marry my sister-in-law. But he never got around to it. He went to California. Left Jimmie Lunceford and went to California and joined up with Harry James. Harry James is one of the [?]readin'est trumpet players I ever saw in my life [laughter]. And can play! But Willie Smith is one of the greatest first alto players you ever heard in your life. Outside of Johnny Hodges. There's a boy. There's a boy that plays melody and he plays swing like a dog. And his notes are truly pure. As I said before, I love beauty, and he's got it. And there's another boy who plays beautiful trombone named Dicky Wells. He was with Basie . . .

So there you are. Them's your boys. We used to

Stuff Smith, Blue Streak and White House, Paris, June 1967

have a good time back in those days. In those days when old . . . Fats Waller [laughter] would be in front of the Music House there on Broadway. And he would say, I'd turn the corner, getting off the subway, and I'd turn the corner, and there would be Fats. And he says Stuff! Draw! So we drew. He would have him a half pint of gin and I'd have me a half pint of gin too. And we drew at each other [laughter]. And he says, let's go somewhere and play . . . So we did. We used to do all that. We had a good time. There's a playing young boy. And a good composer. You know. Those were the days when a musician enjoyed playing. He didn't play for money. He played for himself and for his friends. He was *supposed* to play because it was in his blood. It was in his mind. And in his heart. And in his soul. And in his sleep. And that's what we had. We had the beat in our feet. That's for sure.

And, when Duke wrote this song 'It Don't Mean a Thing if It Ain't Got that Swing' a certain man, a piano player, we call him Willie Slip the Lion [Willie the Lion Smith], he says, now Stuff, that is *right*. It don't mean nothin' if you ain't got nothin' [laughter], somethin'. That means it don't mean a thing if you ain't got that swing. So, we used to go and jam up there in New York, by the Lafayette Theatre. And play until next morning.

Now, there's one man who was really astonishing. He and [Earl] Fatha Hines. Fatha Hines was in Chicago. And this young fella, who was about eighteen years old then, came to Chicago and played *beautiful* piano. The greatest piano I ever heard in my life. He came to Chicago. And Earl Hines says, they tell me you can play piano. So he says, yeah, I can play a little bit [laughter]. So he went on. They went downstairs, A place there in Chicago . . . The Grand Terrace . . . So they went down there. And Earl Hines got on the piano and started playing 'Body and Soul'. And he started playing. So, he played it in D flat, which is five flats, which is the original key. He played it there. And when he finished he says, now, will you play this? He says, yes. But I ain't going to stay in D flat. He says, I'm going to start from C and take it all the way through. C. B flat. B natural. A natural. E natural. G natural. F sharp. *All* them keys I'm going to play it in. And Earl Hines says, aw no. He says, aw yeah. So he sat down. His name was Art Tatum. The greatest pianist that ever lived. Art Tatum. As far as I'm concerned. Yes. Now, that is jazz. That is jazz that you can't forget. That's jazz that stays with you. And will *be* with you as long as you got two feet to stand on. And if you haven't got two feet to stand on you got *one* foot to stand on. But you can still pat that one foot. Believe me. And this boy named Art Tatum could play it. He is one of the greatest musicians that ever lived.

And one of the greatest I ever played with. And I practically played with them all. But he is the boss. He and Duke.

Duke Ellington. One evening, when I got through playing at my club, I was with Charlie Barnet. He's a fine tenor saxophone player. And Charlie says, let's go in, Stuff, and have us a little beer before we go home. I says, sure. And he says, incidentally, old Duke Ellington's playing over here. This was Los Angeles, you know. I says, sure enough [laughter]. So, we went over there. And when we got there Duke was blowing like a dog. Ray Nance was playing the violin. Johnny Hodges was playing the horn. And, my boy [Harry Carney] the baritone. He was playing his baritone. And everything was fine, you know. So I says, Duke, may I play a number with you? He says, sure, Stuff. Come on here. Sit down here and play something. So I went and got my beat up amplifier [laughter] and set up on the stand. Plugged it in, to the socket. And Duke says, C sharp. Now what the hell I know he's talking about C sharp! Well, he says, you got it? C sharp. OK. All right. And we start playing. "C'-Jam Blues'. And we played. We played it for about a half hour. Joe Louis is sitting out in the audience! And he always wanted to be a violin player. Joe Louis. Bless his soul. I love that guy. And so we sat out there and played "C'-Jam Blues'. And I had never played "C'-Jam Blues' like that in my life. Every time I turned round there was another sharp [laughter]. So I got the sharps played.

Oh yeah, that's jazz. Pure jazz. Not this jazz that these cats figure out their way. I mean they stand up there and don't move their body and they don't feel. I don't know how they feel. But to me it looks like it is very *discouraging*. To stand up there and play for audience. And the audience don't know what the hell you're playing. And they stand up there with their feet flat. They've got their horn in their mouth and they

Stuff Smith and Eva Løgager on tour, September 1967

know about three songs. You get them off of them
three songs they don't know *nothing*. That ain't jazz!
Believe me. You'll find that out, later. What I'm telling
you . . . is correct. Ask Timme Rosenkrantz. He
knows. He knows jazz. That's one sure thing about old
Tim. And we love him for that. He knows jazz. There's
a few other boys who know jazz. And when you've got
jazz, you've got it . . .

There's another little fellow, and he's gone away too.
He's one of the finest in the jazz in the country and he
was my friend, very good friend. His name was Hot
Lips Page. He came from Kansas City. A fine trumpet
player and a good singer. And a good entertainer all
the way around.

You know what I should do is tell you about these
boys that I have been speaking about. Well, we start

with, let me see, Henry Red Allen. Henry Red Allen was on the boats in St Louis. Streckfus Steamboat Line with his father. And both of them were playing trumpet, hm. He was on the *J. S.* [ss *J. S. DeLux*]. That's the name of the boat. And Alphonso Trent's band, who I was a member of, we were on the steamer *St Paul*. Now Henry Red Allen's boat used to go to New Orleans. Well, we never went to New Orleans. We'd always go north. And give our little excursion. And every Monday night Louis Armstrong would come from Chicago, and play on the steamer *St Paul*. And we would have us a ball, hm. That cat would come down the street and you thought, ah, President Roosevelt was walking down the street. Everybody enjoyed Louis so much and loved him so much. I just can remember. He had on a camel's hair coat and a camel's hair cap. And he walked up to the steamer, says, boys, and he said, is this it? And we said, yeah, Louis, come on in Pops. And we had a ball that night [laughter].

Now, let me tell you something about Charlie Shavers. I'm taking all the trumpet players now. Charlie Shavers. He's real fast on his horn. And plays fine. He don't miss nothing. And he's a good arranger. As a matter of fact, he kept John Kirby's band going, he and Billy Kyle, for about three years. There's some good arrangers.

Now, let's talk about saxophone players. There's an old beat up fat cat named Ben Webster. He's in Amsterdam now. He's a fine boy. He's like a little baby when he hasn't been drinking. But when he's drinking look out, run, run, you hear me, you run! He's the roughest cat you ever saw in you life, hm. But he's still my pal.

Another tenor saxophone player named Don Stovall. No! I don't mean Don Stovall. I mean Don Byas. Don Stovall is an alto player. He's a good boy. But Don Byas, he and Ben Webster, are in the same class. Only

Don's a little smaller. Don is one of these deep sea divers, who likes to go under the water, with his rubber suit on, and catch fish with a spear [laughter]. I told him, go on down there, Jack, I ain't coming with you. You understand me?

Now, there's another tenor player. His name is Joe Thomas. He used to be with Jimmie Lunceford. And he went to Kansas City and got married. And the girl that he married, her father died and left him a great big block of a funeral parlor. Now, who wants a funeral parlor? But he was there [laughter]! Joe Thomas. There's my boy too. And he can blow.

There's another one. Hal Singer. We can't forget him. He can blow too. Ah yeah. He's here in Paris. He's not playing with me. But he's playing right around the corner. At a place called . . . the Chat qui pêche. I'm saying all these French words. I don't know what the hell they are. But he's a good boy. We're going to play together, the twenty-fourth of this month, in the southern part of France [and in Spain]. That's him.

Now, let me see. There's another tenor player. His name is Ironjaws. From New York. Plays his can off. He was here. [And] at the Montmartre. Did very well in Copenhagen. [? Johnny Griffin, not Eddie Lockjaw Davis.] And he was doing very well. And he did very well. He can blow too.

There's another tenor player, from Little Rock, Arkansas. His name is Hayes Pillars. From the Jeter and Pillars band, hm, hm. He can blow. All them cats can blow. They're solid musicians. They ain't these over the night musicians like you're hearing. You've been brainwashed. That's the trouble with you. All of you have been brainwashed. You little youngsters. You should go back and hear the boys and learn the real jazz. It's true, what I'm saying. And that's the thing that counts. If you want to pat your foot, that's it. This other mess they're laying down, man, I'm sorry.

Now, the swingin'est band, little band, I ever heard in my life, was called the Savoy Sultans. They played at the Savoy Ballroom in New York City. And boy, all them cats could blow like a dog. Yeah . . . And there was another little group called the Five Spirits of Rhythm. Now, Leo Watson was the greatest scat singer you ever heard in your life. That's true. And we used to play together. Yeah, that boy was something.

Now, we'll take Miss Ella Fitzgerald. I gave her her first commercial. On radio. In New York City. Called *Let's Listen to* [?]*Lucidin.* That was eye drops, you know. And Ella Fitzgerald was the vocalist. And our arranger was the fella that wrote 'Stomping at the Savoy'. His name was, hm, I'll think of it and tell you about it later. Anyway, we had half of Chick's band. Chick Webb. We had his brass section. We had Cab Calloway's reed section. Then I had my band stuck in there. Edgar Sampson is that boy's name. That was the arranger of the band. And we had some pretty good arrangements. And we used to hit on that program quite a length of time. So, finally, we made our little loot, and got off of it, and went back to the Onyx Club, to start playing again.

So there you are. One of these days I'm going to tell you about myself. One of these days. How I started in this field of music . . . I just want you to know the boys. And the boys that can really swing. The real boys. Pure at heart, we call them. Pure at heart. So we'll see you later . . .

Recorded by Eva Løgager, Paris, June 1967
Transcribed and edited by Anthony Barnett, October 1990

TIMME ROSENKRANTZ
REFLECTIONS

IN the late 1930s the Onyx Club was the place to go in New York. The clientele was made up mostly of musicians. The host and owner, Joe Helbock, was a former musician and showed good taste in hiring bands.

It was at the Onyx on my first visit to America that I heard the wonderful Spirits of Rhythm. It was here the John Kirby Band was born and where Maxine Sullivan made her debut.

One of the greatest things that happened at the club was the wonderful music of fiddler Stuff Smith and his band, which featured Jonah Jones.

It was at the Onyx that I met Hezekiah Leroy Gordon Smith, a great creative musician who should be placed, I feel, among the top jazz improvisers like Louis Armstrong, Fats Waller, Coleman Hawkins, Art Tatum, and Lester Young. It is significant that all the jazz greats have the highest respect for Stuff, whereas laymen and most jazz fans hardly know him at all.

Being a frustrated but violent violin player myself, I have heard most of the jazz fiddlers from Joe Venuti on; even in little Denmark we have a guy who's a splendid man on fiddle, Svend Asmussen. But Stuff tops them all.

One should hear him *in natura*, this little, nimble fellow, who jumps and dances and almost stands on his head when he plays. He is irresistible—and it is probably only because of his lack of restraint and his more or less bohemian nature, that he isn't better known or even a television star. But with him, one never knows what's going to happen. He is probably the cause of several gray hairs on the heads of many club owners.

I'll never forget him at the Onyx. All of a sudden, while his band was playing, he would disappear and you might find him in either the men's or the ladies' room, playing a pretty solo for the local authority, or he might go to the bar and quench his thirst with a quantity of firewater. Often at the Onyx, after the music started, he would tell *risqué* stories over the microphone. There was one about Adam and Eve in the Garden of Eden, that used to make the management panic.

I've seen him stop in the middle of a solo when a young and beautiful woman entered the room and point out to the audience the woman's anatomical qualities, which remarks sometimes registered unfavorably with her escort. But that didn't stop Stuff. He kept on, and then he would play a dazzling chorus on his violin as if to emphasize what he had just said.

During the war years, Stuff had a little trio—well, it wasn't smaller than any other trio—in fact, one might say it was bigger, because it consisted of Stuff and two wonderful musicians, Jimmy Jones on piano and John Levy on bass.

To my mind, this was one of the finest ensembles jazz has ever given us, and it was a great hit at the Onyx.

Red Norvo and his wife at the time, the wonderful Mildred Bailey, were quite mad about Stuff and his music. Red had a band across 52nd St. at the Downbeat Club, but each intermission he went over to listen to Stuff.

At that time, Mildred had a weekly radio show on CBS. It was more or less a jazz show, and she presented most of the jazz greats, Paul Baron's large orchestra, and, of course, her own inimitable voice. It was quite a show.

Many times she had asked Stuff to play the show. But he was quite shy about it and said he didn't like too many people—she had more than thirty in the band alone [including strings].

But she managed to convince him.

It was arranged that he should come two hours

before the show was to be broadcast so they would have time to rehearse.

There was no Stuff for rehearsal, and Mildred almost went out of her mind. But she kept Baron and everyone waiting to the last minute, and at 8.30—the show's starting time—there was Hezekiah Smith in front of the band, as if he had been shot up through the floor. He played 'Bugle Call Rag' as it never had been played before and never has since. He fell in at all the right places, and the orchestra, audience, and Mildred fell out. [Research suggests that Smith may have been present at the dress rehearsal; two transcription recordings of 'Bugle Call Rag' with Paul Baron and His Orchestra exist—see 'An Interview'.]

Stuff is what one might call a natural musician—he's never taken a lesson [formally, since his childhood]. He just figured it all out by himself, and though he may not play the fiddle the way it was meant to be played, what he does with it is quite fantastic. I often saw old, long-haired symphony men, first violinists from the big radio symphony orchestras, sit at the Onyx and listen carefully to his playing. They were thrilled and fascinated by what they heard, and they asked themselves and everybody else, 'How is it possible? How does he do it?'

Many of them were ready to swap their whole classical training for just a little bit of what Stuff had. [Fritz Kreisler was an ardent admirer and frequent visitor to the Onyx.]

I had an apartment not very far from 52nd St. at that time. Quite often, after the clubs on 52nd St. closed, musicians would come to my place and there would be jamming until the wee hours. A lot of wonderful music was played [some of the music recorded there in the 1940s has been issued], especially by Stuff, who came practically every night.

I had two very comfortable easy chairs. One was for

Stuff to relax in after the sessions . . . and he would be sitting there when I woke up in the afternoon. The house at one time had belonged to Diamond Jim Brady, but when I lived there, it belonged to Stuff Smith.

Stuff's winning personality had endeared him to practically everyone he met, and at this time he was well known at New York radio studios—he had become quite popular at the stations. For instance, here's a wonderful story I was told:

Jascha Heifetz was to play a concert at NBC. He took the main elevator, but the elevator man stopped him when he saw the violin case, and said, 'Sorry, mister. If you are going up to play, you'll have to take the personnel elevator in the back. This one is reserved for the public.'

Heifetz of course was highly insulted and angrily replied, 'My good man, I am sure you don't know who I am. I am Jascha Heifetz!'

To this the elevator man answered, 'Sorry, sir. Even if you were Stuff Smith, you'd still have to take the personnel elevator!'

Reprinted, with editorial insertions, from
Downbeat *3 January 1963*

CHECKLIST

Selected recordings by Stuff Smith issued on LP &/or CD &/or cassette. Some are out of print or are limited editions but, where possible, the most complete and recent issue labels are listed; '*' describes an issue, not necessarily released under the name of the given group, only part of which includes Smith; where two or more issue labels are listed ',' indicates the same session; ';' indicates different sessions. The checklist is a guide to the range of issued recordings by Stuff Smith; it is not complete or critical and is not intended to serve as a discography. A descriptive *Stuff Smith Discography (Disc & Tape),* including 78s and unissued recordings, to which corrections and additions are invited for a definitive edition, is separately available. An album including unissued masterpiece recordings from the 1940s is in preparation.

1928-1930	Alphonso Trent Orchestra	Ristic, *Historical
1936	Teddy Wilson Orchestra	*Jazz Archives
1936-1937	Stuff Smith Onyx Club Boys Affinity;	*Aircheck; *Stash
1939-1940	Stuff Smith Orchestra	*Savoy, *Storyville
1943-1944	Stuff Smith Trio Circle; *Asch; *Fonit-Centra; *Savoy
1944	Stuff Smith, Paul Baron Orchestra	*Swing House
1944	Lucky Thompson, Stuff Smith, Erroll Garner *Swingtime
1945	Stuff Smith Trio	*Mosaic, *Commodore
1945	All Star Band, incl. Duke Ellington	*Jazz Archives
1945	Sarah Vaughan, Stuff Smith Trio	*Musicraft
?1948	Stuff Smith, Sun Ra	*Saturn
1951	Dizzy Gillespie Sextet	*Savoy
1953	Stuff Smith Quartet	*MCA
1956	Ella Fitzgerald	*Verve
1956	Nat King Cole	*Capitol
1956	Nelson Riddle Orchestra	*Capitol
1957	Stuff Smith, Carl Perkins	Verve
1957	Stuff Smith, Oscar Peterson	Verve
1957	Dizzy Gillespie, Stuff Smith	Verve
1957	J.A.T.P.: Stuff Smith Quintet; Ella Fitzgerald	*Tax
1957	Stephane Grappelli, Stuff Smith	Pablo, Fantasy
1957	Billy Daniels, Bennie Payne Orchestra	Verve, HMV
1958	Art Ford TV Jazz Parties	*Jazz Connoisseur
1959	Stuff Smith, Johnny Letman	20th Century Fox
1959	Stuff Smith Quartet	Verve
1963	Herb Ellis, Stuff Smith	Epic
1965	Stuff Smith Quartet Storyville; Storyville, Emarcy
1965	Big Joe Turner	*Europa Jazz
1965	Stuff Smith Groups	France's Concert
1965	Stuff Smith, Stephane Grappelli	Barclay, Everest
1965	Earl Hines All Stars	*France's Concert
1965-1966	Stuff Smith, Svend Asmussen, Poul Olsen Storyville
1966	Violin Summit: S.A., S.G., J.-L.Ponty, S.S. *Saba, *MPS
1967	Stuff Smith Quartet, Quintet Saba, MPS, Prestige

INDEX
(Names other than Hezekiah Stuff Smith)

BARON TIMME ROSENKRANTZ was born in Denmark. His love of jazz took him to New York in 1934. In 1938 he organized a band with which Don Byas first recorded. In the mid-1940s he produced a concert at Town Hall with such musicians as Don Byas, Bill Coleman, Red Norvo, Stuff Smith, and Teddy Wilson. At his apartment he made private recordings of Stuff Smith, in as yet unissued duets with classical pianist Robert Crum, and Erroll Garner. Some of his recordings were issued on the labels Commodore, Selmer, and his own Baronet. In 1946 he arranged for Don Redman to bring the first American orchestra, which included Don Byas, Tyree Glenn, Peanuts Holland and Billy Taylor, to Europe following the war. He published two photo albums *Swing Photo Album* (Copenhagen, 1939, rev.2, London, 1964) and *Jazz Profiles* (Copenhagen, 1945), and a memoir *Dus med jazzen* (Copenhagen, 1965). He brought Stuff Smith to Europe in 1965. He produced a memorial concert for Smith in 1967 which included performances by numerous American and European musicians. The following year he engaged Mary Lou Williams for the opening in Copenhagen of his Timme's Club, where Teddy Wilson also held residencies. He died in 1969 while on a visit to New York.

ANTHONY BARNETT has written the album notes for Storyville, *Stuff Smith, Live at the Montmartre* (STCD 4142) and *Stuff Smith, Hot Violins, with Svend Asmussen and Poul Olsen* (STCD 4170), and, for Affinity, the complete *Stuff Smith and His Onyx Club Boys, Jivin' at the Onyx* (CDAFS 1005). He has published volumes of poetry including *Poem About Music* (Providence, RI, 1974) and, collected, *The Résting Bëll* (London, 1987). He has written about music and literature in *Musics*, on the violinist Leroy Jenkins, *The Guardian* and *The Independent*, and *The New Grove Dictionary of Jazz*. He produced concerts with John Tchicai at the Wigmore Hall in 1968 and in Cambridge in 1969 thereafter broadcasting and recording as a percussionist with Tchicai's Cadentia Nova Danica. He has performed occasionally with such other musicians as Derek Bailey, Don Cherry, Mbizo Dyani, Evan Parker and Leo Smith.

EVA LØGAGER lived together with Hezekiah Stuff Smith in Århus and Copenhagen in Denmark during his last years in Europe, and accompanied him on several tours. She has taken part in radio programs about Smith and makes her home in Horsens, Denmark, near the village where Smith is buried.